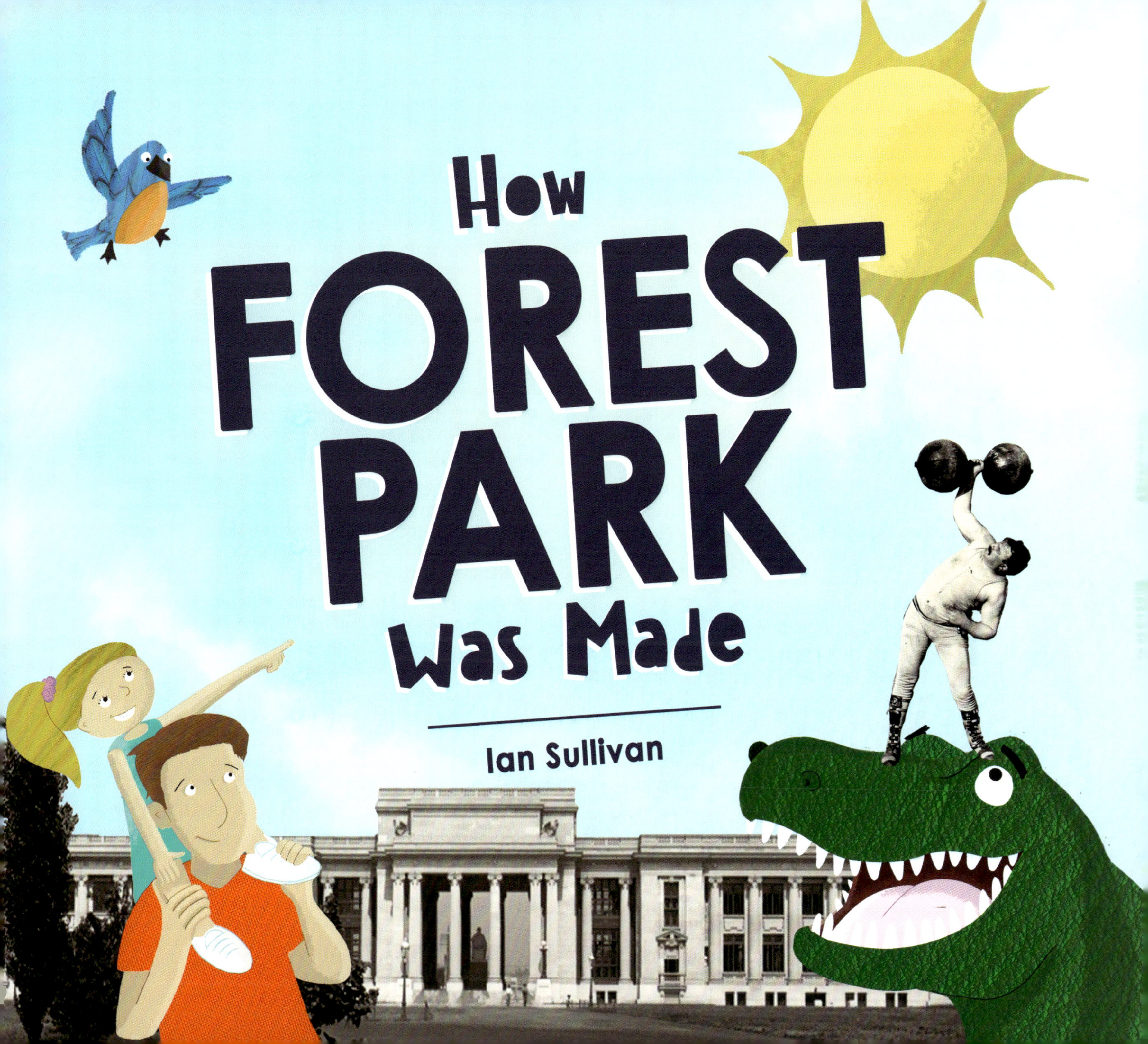

How FOREST PARK Was Made

Ian Sullivan

Reedy Press
PO Box 5131
St. Louis, MO 63139, USA
reedypress.com

ISBN: 9781681066417

Design by Ian Sullivan

Front cover: Photos were provided courtesy of the public domain. Back cover: Muny Cast photo provided by the Muny.

The following photos were provided courtesy of the Missouri Historical Society: Start of Gordon Bennett International Balloon Race, Forest Park (p1, p29); World's Fair Bird Cage in Forest Park (p2); Boy with Toes in Water (p3); Family Picnic (p3); Girl and Boy at Cabanne Spring (p4); World's Fair Ferris Wheel (p5); World's Fair Sign (p5); World's Fair Electric Lights (p6); Steam Train (p6); Fred Winters Olympics (Jessie Tarbox Beals, p7); Olympics Water Sports (p8); Art Hill Sledding (W.C. Persons, p9, p29); Boys on Sled (p10); Washing Elephant (Russell Froelich, p11); Kangaroo (Russell Froelich, p11); Sleeping Bear (p11); Dwight F. Davis. St. Louis Parks Commissioner (p13); Lawn Tennis, Forest Park (Emil Boehl, p13–14); Boys Playing Baseball (p14); Charles Lindbergh Landing the *Spirit of St. Louis* at the Lambert Field After His New York–Paris Flight (Russell Froelich, p15, p29); Team Photo of St. Louis Browns (p16); Girl Scouts Visit the Jewel Box (Howard Vogt, p20); Kids Skating at Steinberg Rink (p23); St. Louis History Program: Forest Park – Planetarium (p23–24); Kids Wrestling in Forest Park, Two Forest Park Mounted Police Officers (James Carrington, p26); Boy Playing Hockey (James M. Carrington, p27).

The following photos were provided courtesy of the *St. Louis Post Dispatch*: Zoo Train (Dorrill Studio) (p12, p29); Wide Shot of People Skating (Ed Burkhardt) (p21); Bonfire Group (p22); Girls Around the Fire (Ed Meyer) (p27).

The following photos were provided courtesy of the Muny: Man & Woman Dancing (p17); Muny Crowd (p17–18); Witch (p18); Actress Giving Autograph (p18); Muny Cast (p28).

The following photos are credited to photographer Stephen Cox: Thomas Jefferson Statue (p15); The Jewel Box Exterior (p19); Planetarium (p23-24); The Boathouse Exterior (p26); Saint Louis Art Museum (p27).

Unless otherwise noted, all other photos are courtesy of the author or believed to be in the public domain.

Printed in Canada
26 27 28 29 30   5 4 3 2 1

REEDY PRESS

Dedication

For Deanna & our kids—who make everywhere the ultimate destination

And for Mom—who filled voids with adventure, including Forest Park

Welcome to Forest Park.

There's so much to explore. Animals, rocket ships, balloon races, and more.

This ultimate playground
for everyone to share . . .
is lively and grand but started . . .

simple & spare.

The park opened to St. Louis in 1876.
Crowds enjoyed clean air as they . . .

mingled & mixed.

It hosted a fair, lasting seven months long.
Palaces and inventions and . . .

that famous old song.

Kids ate their first hot dogs and drank their first iced teas. Electricity gave power to . . . **lights & machines.**

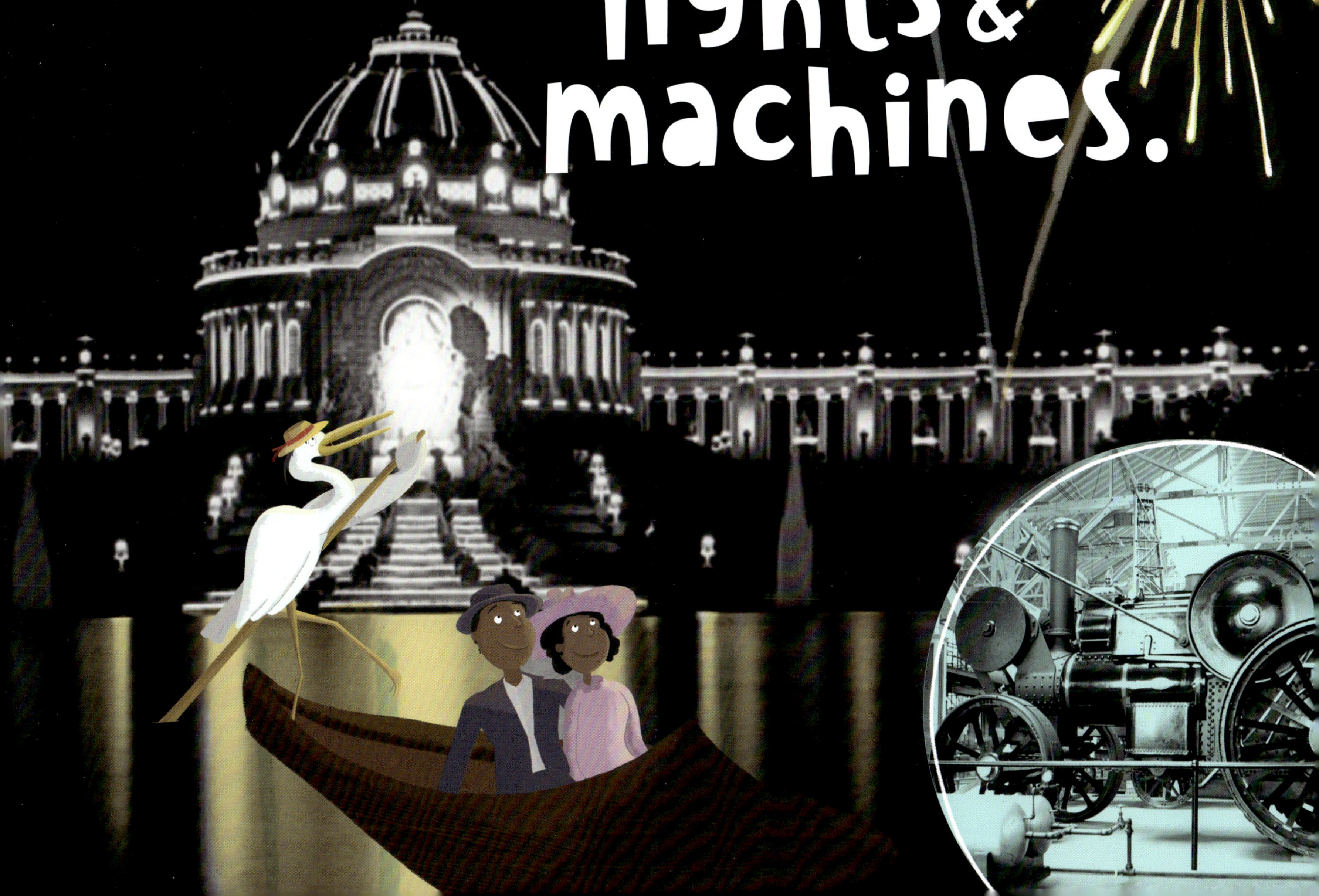

Among the festivities . . .

the Olympics held sway.

Water sports filled lakes during . . .

action-packed days.

The city gained a museum perched above Art Hill.
Inside, paintings grace the halls, while . . .

outside, people chill.

In 1910, the park added a zoo. Soon came . . .

crocodiles, koalas & red kangaroos.

Riding the train, every passenger can see . . .

animals playing in pits, dens & trees.

When Dwight Davis took charge,
he pushed for more sports . . .

ballfields,
a golf course

and new tennis courts.

Prefer archery or hoops?
There is space for that, too.

To **shoot, drive, or dribble** . . . whatever you do.

Around the same time,

a new museum came to be,

on people and events of . . .

our state's history.

Along came a theater, but the stage was outside.

Thousands packed the Muny,

the first of its kind.

Performers still dazzle in the glow of the lights, entertaining St. Louis on warm summer nights.

The 1930s brought . . . the Jewel Box with its giant glass walls.

Housing palm trees and flowers,

it stands

50 feet tall.

Etta Steinberg saw an ice rink in New York's Central Park.

She had one built to . . .

enjoy in both daylight & the dark.

Bring your own blades
or rent them to skate.

And afterwards . . .

hot cocoa &
a fire await.

The Planetarium first

looked like it landed from space.

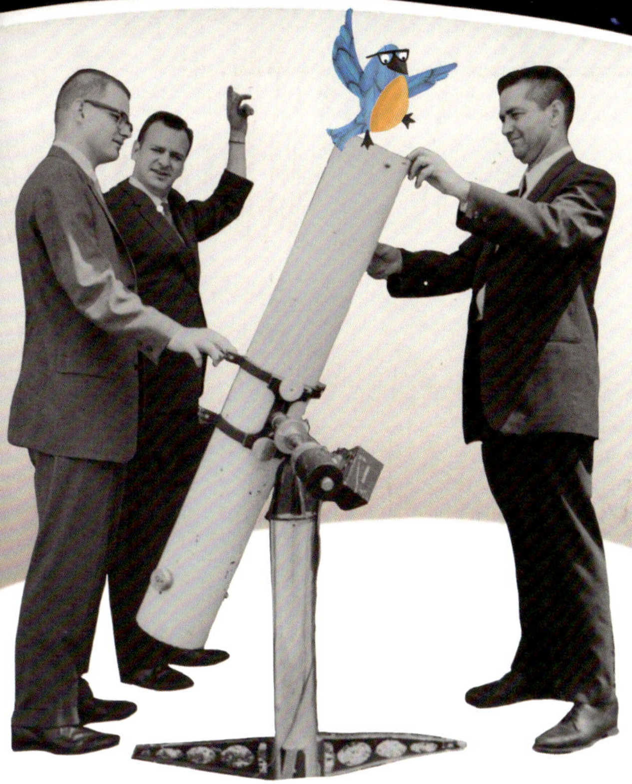

Images of the heavens

. . . could be viewed in one place.

Forest Park is a wonderland . . .

and that we all see.
Natural beauty abounds
in the lakes and the trees.

Through 150 years . . .

it has become even more.
Imagination and effort
brought activity galore.

The park's here all year.
Drop by December

or June.

Enjoy your next visit,
then come back again soon.

Fun Facts About Forest Park

Nothing & a Nickel

One reason the city picked Forest Park as the home for our free zoo was because it could be reached by anyone for just five cents carfare.

Four-Legged Sledding

The first sled trips down Art Hill were by World's Fair employees on folding chairs.

Look, a Star-splosion!

The planetarium can project 9,000 stars. That's way more than we can see outside on a given night.

Mmm . . . Electric Cand

The World's Fair showcased an earl electric cotton candy machine. Onc visitors realized it truly was candy, it was an instant hit.

Floating the Distance

The winner of the 1907 balloon race floated for 40 hours from Forest Park to New Jersey. That's a distance of 873.4 miles!

Hillside Hero's Welcome

100,000 people jammed onto Art Hill to greet Charles Lindbergh after he made our city world-famous by flying the *Spirit of St. Louis* from New York to Paris.